Contents

Acknowledgements
Text by Loel Collins.
The publishers would like to thank
Pyranha Mouldings Limited and Palm
Canoe Products Limited for their
contribution to this book.

All photographs by Heather Gunn, except
for: front cover (courtesy of Michael
Durham); page 7 (Allsport UK Ltd); page
48 (Robert Johnson).
Illustrations by Margaret Jones.

Note   Throughout the book paddlers
are referred to individually as 'he'. This
should, of course, be taken to mean 'he
or she' where appropriate.

Getting started

Kayak canoeing is a fantastic sport. It offers a great variety of experiences that can suit anyone irrespective of age, sex or ability. It has developed greatly over the last ten years: new materials, new designs and new attitudes have led to a rapid increase in standards. Boats are now designed with the recreational 'paddler' in mind. No longer hindered by the regulations of competition, boats are specifically designed to meet the demands of an ever increasing number of people of all ages and sexes who find something special about kayak canoeing.

The increase in numbers of paddlers has led to an increase in the variety and designs of modern clothing. Long gone are the days of plimsolls and shorts; now there are designer wetsuits, specialist dry cags, and stylish buoyancy aids. More people want to be comfortable and warm in their sport, and the clothing manufacturers have responded.

With the correct supervision and knowledge of the basic safety principles, kayaking is safe and great fun. Once you've caught the bug, there's no looking back.

For your first sessions you will need very little more than a swimming costume, old trainers, tracksuit bottoms and a warm, long-sleeved top. If it's cool you may need a waterproof top and trousers. Your paddle, buoyancy aid and boat should all be provided. After your outing it is a good idea to have a warm set of clothes to change into. Don't forget to take a towel.

The buoyancy aid

This is a waistcoat filled with buoyant foam. It should be comfortable to wear, it should not restrict your breathing or movement and it should have a waist tie. Before you put it on, quickly glance over it to make sure there are no rips or tears in it and that the zip, if it has one, is working. Make sure that the waist tie is serviceable. Place the buoyancy aid on over your clothes and jacket, checking that the zip is pulled right up and the waist tie fastened.

The paddle

Your choice of paddle is very important. Bear in mind that the demands you make on your paddle will change as you develop your paddling skill. At first you will want a light, relatively short paddle that is easy to handle. On first picking it up you will notice that the blades are set at different angles – this is known as the *feather* and dictates whether the paddle is left- or right-handed.

To check whether the paddle is suitable for you, stand it next to your foot and reach up to the top blade with the same hand; the top edge of the blade should be level with your wrist. To ensure that the blades are feathered properly, stand the paddle in front of you, making sure that the bottom blade's curved face – the *drive face* – is towards you. The top blade's drive face faces the right if the paddle is right-handed and vice versa.

Pick up the paddle with your hands shoulder-width apart, holding it evenly as if you were riding a bike. Rotate the paddle in your hands until the top edge of the blade closest to your dominant hand lines up with your knuckles. A slight oval in the loom will help you to find the correct position.

▲ *A simple buoyancy aid*

Holding the paddle correctly is a very ▶
important early skill

5

The boat

Your first boat will probably be made of roto-moulded plastic and be very tough, so the inevitable bumps of your initial sessions won't matter. Modern kayaks have several safety features that you should check before going on to the water. At the ends of the kayak there should be a toggle to help you to carry the boat. Most boats now have a 'keyhole' cockpit which allows you to enter and exit from the boat easily. Behind the cockpit, a solid foam pillar supports the back deck. In front of the cockpit the space for your legs should be kept clear, containing only a footrest. Beyond this, a second foam block provides further flotation.

Getting afloat

Before you go on to the water, your instructor will want to go through a couple of safety points with you:

● he will set limits to the area in which you can paddle in at first
● he will take you through the theory of the capsize.

A note on capsizing

Capsizing can happen, but it should be viewed as a possibility rather than a probability. Should your boat turn over, it is very easy to get out. A swimming pool is the ideal place to practise your capsize, and clubs and centres will often use a pool for your first session.

If you do go over, don't worry. It may be the first time but it will probably not be the last. Remember that getting wet isn't a problem – it's fun!

● Once you are upside-down, place your hands opposite your hips on the boat. Simply straighten your legs and push your bottom off the seat.
● As you leave the kayak, gently roll forwards. As you come up to the surface you will be greeted by cheers from your fellow students and the smiling face of your instructor who will have you back in your boat in no time.

A couple of things make life easier for your instructor:

● try to keep hold of your paddle and boat
● leave the boat upside-down; this traps a pocket of air inside it and makes it easier to empty.

Getting into a kayak is straightforward; just make each movement gentle and controlled.

● Lift the kayak into the water, keeping your paddle close at hand and making sure that the boat is facing upstream.

● Crouch on the bank facing the front of the boat. Place the paddle across the bank and boat and then grasp the front of the cockpit in one hand, keeping the other on the bank. Lean forwards, distributing your weight evenly between both arms.

● Keeping your weight over your arms, gently step one foot into the centre of the kayak (in front of the seat). Still keeping your weight over the paddle, bring the other foot in and gently sit down.

● Straighten your legs out against the footrest. Your knees should be braced underneath the thigh braces.

● Pick up your paddle with the correct grip and gently push yourself from the bank.

▲ *Make sure the kayak is afloat and that your paddle is close at hand*

▼ *Place the paddle across the boat and bank*

▲ *Keeping your weight over the paddle, step gently into the centre of the boat*

◀ *Once sitting down, place your knees under the braces and put your toes against the footrest. Pull the paddle in front of you*

Your instructor will get on to the water before you. It may take some time to get everyone afloat; don't waste the time. Your first 10 minutes in a boat are very important: you will learn a lot in a very short time. Try a few games!

● Throw your paddle on to the water in front of you; use your hands to move yourself over to retrieve it.
● Spin the paddle around your head.
● Holding the paddle normally, place the blade in the water, close your eyes and try moving the blade through the water. At times it will feel like slicing through butter; at others it will feel as if it is being pulled through treacle. Do this gently at first.
● Try using the paddle to push yourself forwards, backwards, to the left and to the right. You will move further if you twist the paddle.
● Sit in the boat and lift one knee so that the boat rises up on that side. Hold that knee up and then gently relax it. Try the same with the other knee.
● Lean forwards and then backwards towards the stern of your kayak. Try to place your head on the front deck and then on the rear deck.

These games, which comprise only a few simple experiments in moving your body, boat and blade, can rapidly build up your confidence and help you to learn. Any movement should be performed carefully, keeping your centre of gravity inside the boat.

▲ *By moving your head 'outside' the boat. you become off-balance*

▼ *By keeping your head 'inside' the boat, you can stay balanced – but still move your hips*

Forward paddling

Once everyone is afloat your instructor will show you how to paddle. Building on the games outlined previously, you will be able to learn very easily how to paddle.

● Holding your paddle lightly with the correct grip (*see* page 5), reach forwards with the right-hand blade as far as you can. The best reach is obtained by twisting from your hips rather than *leaning* forwards.
● Place the blade by pushing the paddle into the water with your top hand. Once immersed, start to pull the blade through the water parallel to the boat with your lower hand, while guiding the top of the paddle with your upper hand.
● As the right-hand blade reaches your hip, lift the blade from the water by bending your elbow. The left-hand blade will be feathered automatically at the correct angle, so that it can be pushed easily into place.

● Pull the left-hand blade through the water.
● As the left-hand blade reaches your hip, lift it from the water and place the right-hand blade back into the water. As you do this, relax your right wrist; this allows the blade to fall back into the water at the best angle.

This is basic forward paddling. At first the boat will appear to have a mind of its own, but you will find that steering it is straightforward. The more correction you need, the lower the paddle action. By sweeping the blade away from the boat you can get the boat to turn more. Ideally, this correcting action needs to start at the front of the boat and on the inside of the turn.

If the paddle is swept away from the boat in a wide arc, with the blade just under the surface of the water, the kayak will turn abruptly and through a large angle.

By keeping the arm that is closer to the blade in the water straight, and the path of the paddle wide, a very effective correction can be made.

As you paddle off and the boat moves off-line, listen to the back of the boat; you can hear it skid across the surface of the water as the kayak spins. It is the *stern* of the boat that creates the problem, so a further refinement to this *sweep stroke* would be to use just the last half of the sweep. Care should be taken to ensure that the lower arm is kept straight. Twisting from the hips to follow the paddle makes life a good deal easier.

Note These instructions are written as if the paddler is right-handed. If you are left-handed, simply reverse the instructions. A mirror image is created.

▲ Place the blade by pushing the paddle into the water with your top hand. Once immersed, start to pull the blade through the water, parallel to the boat, with your lower hand, while guiding the top of the paddle with your upper hand

▲ As the right-hand blade reaches your hip, lift the blade from the water by bending your elbow. The left-hand blade will be feathered automatically at the correct angle, so that it can be pushed easily into place by the left hand

◄ Pull the left-hand blade through the water

13

▲ *A high paddle action pushes the boat forwards*

▲ *A low paddle action spins the boat*

14

▲ *Starting close to the feet*

▲ *Keep the arm straight and the paddle away from the boat*

*The full
sweep stroke*

◄ *Sweep the blade towards
the back of the boat*

15

The next stages

After your first couple of sessions you will know if kayaking is for you. You should then start to consider buying your own equipment.

The array of equipment available is often confusing, with a wide variety of colours and designs. The main thing to remember is that your clothing should keep you comfortable and warm.

Clothing

Most kayakers dress themselves in wetsuit boots, wetsuit, dry cag, thermal top, spray deck, buoyancy aid and a helmet and carry a throw line if they are intending to venture on to white water.

Wetsuits

Modern wetsuits are made of soft and supple *neoprene* and come in a wide variety of designs and colours. They work by trapping a layer of water close to the skin; the water is then warmed by the body's natural temperature.

A good fit is essential. 'Long John' style suits with enough room for the arms to move freely are ideal. A full diving suit restricts movement. The suit should fit you snugly whilst you are sitting down: too tight, and your movement can be restricted; too loose, and the suit will not keep you warm because the water is continually flushed through it.

Wetsuit boots are a real luxury. A good fit is essential, and the sole should protect your feet as you walk down river banks. The boots quickly start to smell, so regular washing is essential. Sports sandals are a great alternative and don't smell, but they are rather cool on a cold day.

Dry cag

This is a simple, short waterproof jacket that keeps out the worst of the water. The wrists are sealed with either neoprene cuffs or latex rubber seals; similar seals at the neck and a neoprene cuff at the waist all make the dry cag quite an effective garment.

Thermal top

Many kayakers wear a swimming costume and thermal top under the cag and wetsuit. A simple, long-sleeved polypropylene top is enough in summer. In the winter, a bulkier fleece top is more suitable.

Spray deck

This is a cockpit cover, made of nylon or neoprene and designed to keep the water out of the boat. It fastens around the cockpit rim with elastic. A strap at the front allows you to release this if you capsize. It is a good idea to practise your capsize a couple of times to make sure that you are familiar with the release mechanism. Make sure you are supervised.

Buoyancy aid

The range of buoyancy aids on the market is enormous. One that is specially designed for kayaking is ideal. It should be comfortable when you are sitting down and come to the bottom of your rib cage. Pockets are handy for odds and ends. Some buoyancy aids have safety harnesses; these are very specialised rescue tools and training is essential before you buy one.

All buoyancy aids should have a waist tie. The flotation in the jacket will decrease as the buoyancy aid ages and you will need to replace it every two or three years.

Helmet

If you intend to venture on to moving water, you must wear a helmet. This is a plastic shell filled with dense foam that can be cut to fit your head. The shell should come well down over your forehead and also cover the base of your skull. A solid buckle is needed for the chin strap, and this needs to be well attached to the helmet. Take time to fit the helmet; once it is on you should not be able to lift the front of it up your forehead.

Throw line

This is a small bag of floating line, brightly coloured and about 8 mm in diameter, that can be thrown to someone in the water. The thrower retains the other end of rope and pulls the swimmer to shore.

▲ *A suitable first layer: sports sandals, wetsuit, Long Johns, spray deck, thermal top*

▲ *Fully kitted with a helmet, dry cag and buoyancy aid*

17

Choosing a paddle

This can be a complex business, but it is worth spending time to ensure that you get the best paddle for you. Paddles come in measured lengths, all around the 2 m mark. You will often hear the paddle length abbreviated to '200', meaning a 2 m paddle, or '206', meaning a paddle that is 2.06 m long.

If you do not know what length of paddle you used before, don't worry. Measure the paddle as before (*see* page 5). If you are paddling for recreation on flat water, you may need a paddle that you can curl your finger tips over at the top; if you are progressing to moving water, a shorter paddle that reaches below your wrist may be more suitable for your requirements.

Until now you will have been using a *symmetrical* blade; however, an *asymmetric* blade offers better performance. Until recently these blades were very light and fragile, but several companies now make heavier duty asymmetric blades that are ideal for beginners but have the performance of a competition blade.

The feather of the blade can vary considerably. Try out several paddles until you find a feather that you find comfortable. Contrary to popular belief, the feather of a paddle is not set at 90° – if you flex your wrist back it will not move enough to accommodate such an extreme feather. Feathers of around 80° or even 70° are often used; you should try as many as you can before you make a decision.

Spend a little time considering the loom (the shaft between the two blades). It should have a slight oval to facilitate the grip of your controlling hand. Some paddlers also have an oval for their non-controlling hand. The diameter of the loom is also important: if you have ever had wrist problems it may well be worth looking around for smaller paddle looms.

Symmetric blade ▲

▲ *Asymmetric blade*

Your boat

The best thing to do is to try out as many boats as possible. Watch people of the same age, size, sex and ability as yourself and ask yourself the following questions.

- Does the boat fit them?
- Are they in control?
- Does it have all the necessary safety features?

If the answer to all these questions is yes, you should have a good long go in a comparable boat. Then ask yourself a few more questions.

- Is it comfortable?
- Can I paddle it in a controlled fashion?
- Did I get off the water smiling?

When choosing a boat, colour can be important – you should be visible if you capsize. Think too about the type of plastic. Most boats are now made of plastic; only specialised boats are made of high-tech composites and these are much more expensive. Plastic boats are mostly roto-moulded in either a linear or a cross-linked plastic. The cross-linked type is stronger but it is harder to repair if broken. Some kayaks are blow-moulded and so are extremely strong, but they are heavy and lack the design refinements of roto-moulded boats.

Once you have decided which boat to buy, borrow or beg, you can then start to develop your kayaking skills.

Fitting your boat

You must use your hips, thighs, knees and feet to drive the boat. Sit in your boat, on dry land, and make sure that you are comfortable in the seat. Raise your knees so that they are held underneath the braces; you will need to adjust the footrest so that it allows you to sit in the correct position. The balls of your feet against the footrest will allow you to flex your ankles and hold yourself in position, whilst relaxing them will allow you to rest your knees. Your hips may be loose in the boat; gluing pads on to the seat can help. The time spent fitting your boat is well spent and can really help your paddling.

▲ *Hip pads, backrest, knee braces: vital to fit the boat. Airbags are also fitted*

Refining your kayaking skills

Watch good paddlers for long enough and you will quickly notice that their actions are smooth, efficient and 'seamless' – everything blends into one fluent sequence so that only momentary pauses allow you to identify individual strokes. Try to see the paddling action as one continuous movement.

Refining your technique into a skilful and controlled combination of blade, boat and body movement is an important and continuous process. You may find the following series of games and exercises helpful.

Exploring the possibilities

● Get into your boat, on the water. Gently lift one knee so that it raises the edge of the boat. Try to keep sitting upright – you can hold the boat up with your hand. Then, gently lower your knee and allow the boat to flatten out. Repeat this exercise on the other side.

● Sitting in your boat, reach forwards with your right-hand paddle. Try to achieve this by rotating your shoulders rather than leaning forwards, as an upright posture is important. As you reach forwards you should feel a slight increase in pressure on your right foot against the footrest. Paddle forwards; as you reach forwards with the left-hand blade you should feel a similar pressure with your left-hand foot. Imagine a searchlight strapped to the front of your buoyancy aid – as you paddle forwards, shine this light from side to side.

● Paddle for a while with a high paddle action. You will quickly notice that the boat veers away from the paddle stroke. To compensate for this, lower the paddle action into a sweep to stroke on the other side.

● Having experimented with the knees, a couple of simple games can help you to refine your boat control skills. Paddle a figure-of-eight course, trying to use only forward paddling strokes. This will be difficult at first! Now paddle the same course, but try to lift the outside edge of the boat as you turn. To do this, you will have to sit on the buttock on the inside of the turn.

The stern of the boat should 'carve' into the turn rather than skid.

▲ *Using your hands to help at first will encourage you to use the hips more* ▲

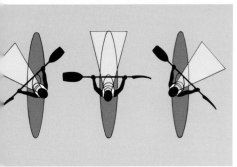

▲ *Fig. 1 Trunk rotation is crucial. Notice the different angles of the light beam which indicate the rotation of the paddler's trunk*

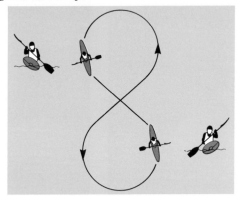

▲ *Fig. 2 Paddling a figure-of-eight circuit*

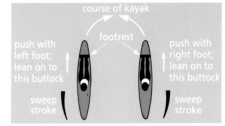

▲ *Fig. 3 Use of the legs inside the boat. One result of driving the boat around corners is that the outside edge of the kayak is often lowered. While using the outside foot to drive, you should also lean slightly on to the buttock on the inside of the turn, thus keeping the outside edge of the boat raised*

21

Balancing the boat

During these exercises the boat may well feel unbalanced. A simple recovery can be achieved by using the back of the blade against the water. As you feel the boat move off-balance, hold the paddle out at right angles to the boat by resting the back of the blade on the surface of the water and pushing down. This will bring the boat back upright. The blade will dive beneath the surface and will need to be recovered by slicing it back up to the surface. As you push down on the blade, lift up the edge of the boat on that side – almost as if you are trying to bring your knee and hand together.

This works well in the case of a slight imbalance. Should the boat move further off-balance, you will need a more substantial support stroke. The drive face can be used by holding the paddle at chest height with your elbows below the loom. As you move off-balance, extend the arm closer to the water so that the blade lands flat on the surface. As the blade strikes the surface, pull it down and pull the same knee upwards. Try to keep your top hand close to the boat and avoid pushing the hand either upwards or forwards.

Don't be afraid to experiment! At worst you will only get wet, but at best you can find new ways of controlling your kayak.

▲ *Set up for the low brace*

▲ *A high brace in action*

Paddle stroke varieties

Imagine you are sitting, in your boat, in the middle of a huge pizza. The pizza is cut into six equal slices. This will help you to visualise the positions and movements involved in each different paddle action.

Paddle movements within each section will have different effects on the boat. Paddle strokes in the front two portions will have most effect on the bow of the boat, whilst in the mid-portions low, wide strokes will have a turning effect. High, close strokes will push the boat forwards. Strokes at the stern can be used to steer the back of the kayak.

Paddle strokes in front of you can be either vertical or low, whilst strokes behind will need to be low to be effective. Provided that the boat is moving, some strokes can be held momentarily to create turns or to steer the kayak. These can be carried out either in the front slices of the pizza or in the two closest to the stern of the boat.

Fig. 4 Imagine your boat is in the middle of a huge pizza ▶

Whilst you experiment, close your eyes and move the paddle through the water. At times it will feel like slicing through butter, yet at others it will feel as if it is being pulled or pushed through syrup. Try holding the paddle in your finger tips; you will feel the blade wobble as it is pulled through the water. As you paddle forwards, release the finger on your top hand so that you are pushing with only the pads of your palm, then try releasing the thumb of your lower hand so that you pull the paddle with only your fingers around the loom. Try combining the two, pushing with the pads of the top hand whilst pulling with the fingers of your lower hand.

Figs 5–9 on pages 25–9 show five simple exercises that will help you to improve your blade awareness and paddle control skills.

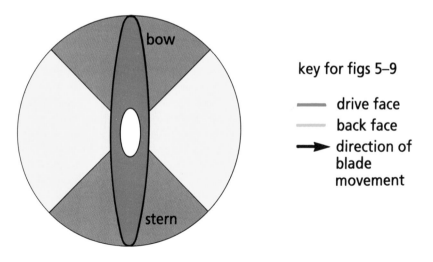

key for figs 5–9

⸺ drive face
⸺ back face
➜ direction of blade movement

▲ *A low stroke at the bow*

▲ *A high stroke at the bow*

▲ *A low steering stroke at the stern*

▲ *A relaxed grip allows you to 'feel' the paddle more*

Exercise 1

Try this without moving the kayak at first (*see* fig. 5). Place the blade in the water behind you with the drive face towards the boat, then slice it from behind you towards the bow. As you slice forwards, lift your front hand, bringing the paddle to the vertical. Once the paddle is upright, slice the blade out along the cut in the pizza. When your lower arm is almost straight, hold the blade in position, keeping it in the water and the drive face facing towards the kayak.

Once you have mastered this on both sides, experiment with the same action on the move. It will create a turn towards the side of the paddle. A further refinement would be to perform only the final part of the stroke, pushing the blade out along the cut line without the slice from behind.

Fig. 5 Exercise 1 ▷

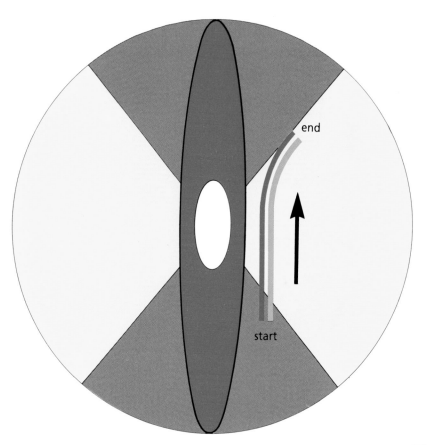

25

Exercise 2

The second exercise builds on the first (*see* fig. 6). From the finishing point of the first exercise, draw the paddle towards the bow of the kayak. As the blade reaches the hull, twist it round so the drive face is towards you. Finish with a power stroke. This will create a turn similar to the first but the draw can be used to increase the amount of turn and the power stroke will push you off in the new direction.

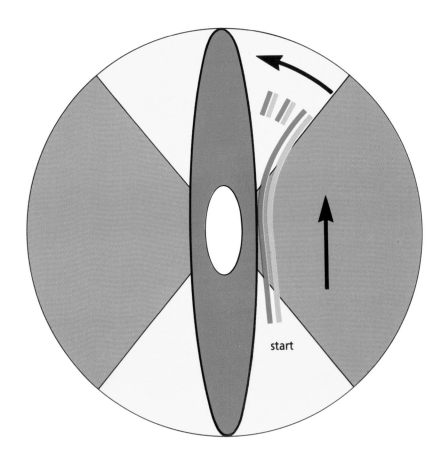

start

Fig. 6 Exercise 2 ▶

26

Exercise 3

This stroke is a very effective correcting action for when the boat moves off-line (*see* fig. 7). It can equally be added to the second, and even the first and the second together with practice (*see* figs 5–6).

As the power stroke reaches your hip, slice the blade out along the second cut line until your lower arm is straight. At the same time, lower your upper arm to bring the paddle down; finish with a wide, low stroke towards the stern of the kayak, keeping your arm straight and using your body to twist.

By linking exercises 1, 2, and 3 you will create the combined effects of both the first and second exercises but you will also turn the kayak away from the paddle at the end of the sequence – making the shape of an 'S'.

Fig. 7 Exercise 3 ▶

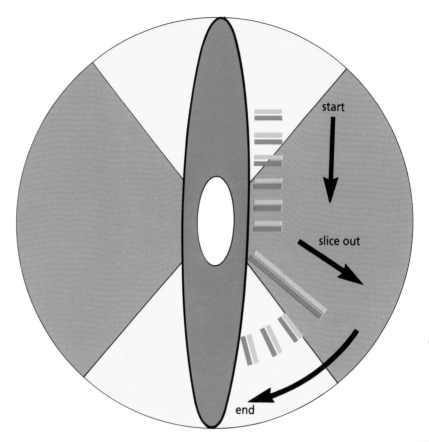

Exercise 4

This exercise builds on a basic sweep stroke (*see* fig. 8). It starts from the rear of the kayak. Twist round so you can reach the stern of the boat with your paddle. Keep your arm straight and sweep the paddle out and towards the bow of the boat; the blade needs to stay just under the surface.

As the blade moves opposite your hip, twist the paddle so your wrists drop below the paddle loom. This will twist the blade. Continue the sweep towards the bow, still keeping the lower arm straight. This front portion of the stroke is rather ineffective and can be improved by raising your top hand – gradually – until by the time the blade reaches the boat you are dangling the paddle from your top hand.

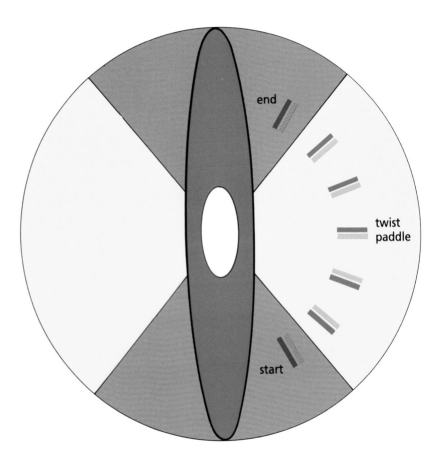

Fig. 8 Exercise 4 ▶

Exercise 5

This exercise is ideal for learning to change the angle of the blade slightly (*see* fig. 9). It can then be co-ordinated with large blade movements. Start as for the last exercise but hold the blade flat on the surface of the water, drive face down. Skim the blade towards the front of the boat. Just as the blade reaches the bow, twist the blade slightly so you can skim it back towards the stern. As the blade reaches the stern subtly twist it again so that you repeat the action.

Once you can sweep the blade forwards and backwards without it diving under the water, you can go one of two ways. Still skimming back and forth, lean towards the blade in the water. You can get a surprising degree of support in this way – a good stunt but not really a useful stroke. Alternatively, still skimming, raise your top hand until you are dangling the paddle from your top hand. The boat should be drawn smoothly sideways, provided that you keep those changes in blade angle subtle.

Fig. 9 Exercise 5 ▶

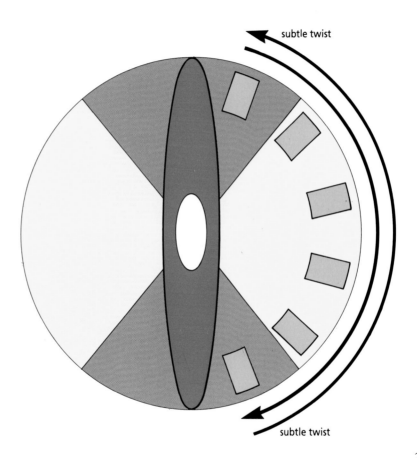

subtle twist

subtle twist

A good exercise ▶

*A sculling draw in ▶
action*

In front and behind you

We have already recognised that strokes can be either *low* or *high*, and also that strokes can be either *moving* – a low, wide sweep stroke that pushes or pulls the boat, for example – or *static*, relying on the movement of the boat through the water to create the effect. A good example of a static stroke is the bow rudder (*see* photo bottom right).

At the moment it is best to consider that any stroke behind you is a low stroke, created with good body movement rather than arm movement, whilst in front of you high strokes are created by 'dangling' the paddle from the top hand. In this way it hangs vertically into the water whilst the lower arm positions the blade in the water.

Practise these on your left and right side alternately. On your non-dominant side you should try to create a mirror image. This may feel awkward at first; it helps if you use your dominant hand to present the blade correctly to the water at the start of the exercise, then use the hand closer to the water to do all the 'fine' control. As you do this you will need to relax your dominant hand to let the blade move

Dangle the paddle from your top arm ▶

A good bow rudder will turn the boat with little loss of speed ▶

freely. Use both hands to control the paddle; if one hand is controlling, the other will need to be relaxed to allow the blade to move.

As you do these exercises you will notice the kayak turn and move. These blade movements are fundamental to kayak control and should be practised with the boat stationary before starting to experiment with them on the move. Begin gently and gradually increase the speed.

Rolling a kayak

Increasing access to swimming pools for kayakers has meant that rolling is no longer the privilege of a select few. Clubs spend many winter evenings running introductory rolling sessions in the comfortable environment of a swimming pool.

The roll is not a hard skill to learn but it does require an open mind. The sensation is quite odd, and the fact you are upside-down in the water adds an extra stress that often inhibits people and prevents them from picking up this skill sooner. Water confidence is vital and the support of a willing partner essential. Outlined overleaf is a basic rolling progression that has developed from the simplest teaching methods employed in the USA, New Zealand and the UK.

● Once you are happy with your capsize and exit from your boat, enlist the help of a willing partner. If you want to be recovered once you have capsized, simply bang on the bottom of your kayak. This is the signal for your partner to reach over your upturned kayak and grasp the cockpit rim. He then keeps his arms straight and leans back to bring you upright. Provided that you lean forwards you can be recovered easily.

● The basis of a good roll is flexibility in the hips. Sit up and lift your right knee, then relax it and lift your left knee; the boat will rock from side to side but you should stay balanced.

● Now lie on the rear deck of the boat and try copying that action. The only way to get the boat to rock is to move your upper body from side to side. This often unbalances you so you have no chance of a really effective recovery.

● Having established that your hips work best for you if you are sitting up, you then need to encourage your body to move as if rolling. The exercise used by most enlightened Coaches is as follows.

Lean forwards with both hands on the left-hand side of the boat. If you are leaning forwards enough you will probably capsize to that side. Stay in that position until your hands reach the surface. Once you feel air, gradually sweep your hand out and down towards the bottom of the pool. As you do this, sit up then gradually sweep your hands back towards the surface until you are leaning forwards again with your hands out of the water on the other side of the kayak. A quick tap on the hull and your partner will pull you up. Repeat this until it becomes a smooth and fluent action. Ideally your partner should stand on the side you are capsizing towards; your recovery will then produce the sensation of a full roll.

● Again with your partner on the same side, capsize. As your hands appear on the other side of the boat, get your partner to roll you up slowly so that the movement matches the speed of your sweeping action. If this is done correctly your hands should stay on the surface of the water. Encourage yourself to look down as you come up.

Once you are both working together and producing consistent results, get your partner to stand on the other side of the boat. As your hands appear, allow him to take your hands and sweep them out as for the previous exercise; if you continue the movement you will find yourself upright. Get your partner to give you a score to indicate the amount of pressure you put on his hands – 0 is no pressure, 5 indicates that you were lifted upright. Practise until you are consistently scoring 1. If you score 0 you are *hand rolling*.

● Now you can introduce the paddle. Move your partner back to the original side. As you capsize, get him to place a paddle over the upturned hull so that it sticks out at 90°. Make sure the wet blade is flat on the surface of the water, grasp the paddle normally and perform the exercise again.

Practise this until you are happy and then hold the paddle as you go over. It will be a lot easier if the paddle is alongside the boat (on the side you are capsizing towards). Make sure you are leaning forwards. Keep the paddle alongside the boat until you are fully over, and as your hands feel the air push both hands further out of the water. Swing the paddle out so that the blade in front of you moves out opposite you and the one behind you moves over the boat. Once the blade is out, gently tap it on the surface of the water to make sure you feel some resistance. If not, twist the paddle so you do feel resistance, and then run through the whole series of exercises. You have now performed a roll – well done!

Reaching over the upturned boat ▶

▲ *Leaning back to recover the kayak*

▲ A good exercise for your hips
▼ Laying back limits your hip mobility

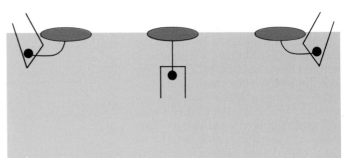

▲ Fig. 10 Note the body movement required to perform an effective roll. Left: *reaching to the surface on the left of the boat – arms reach out of the water, back arches in that direction, noticeable bend in the spine is evident.* Centre: *sitting upright in the boat with the hands towards the bottom of the pool, arms outstretched and the spine straight.* Right: *mirror image of left-hand figure*

▼ Capsize towards your partner

▲ *Assistance from your partner to sweep your hands out*

▲ *Correct paddle position is vital*

Your first roll ▶

35

Competition

Slalom

Kayak slalom is an exciting white-water challenge demanding precise boat control and a good understanding of the white-water environment. Races usually take place over a course of 400–600 m, often on white water but in the lower divisions on calmer rivers. A series of 25 gates are hung over the river and the kayaker weaves a path through the gates attempting not to touch them. If he does, extra time is added to the total time for the course. Male and female categories are usually contested, with a system of six divisions. Competitors can progress through from division 5 to the premier division.

Sprint racing

Sprint racing is an opportunity to pit kayaker against kayaker over a short, flat water course. Regattas are held around the country and often hosted by one of the clubs specialising in sprint racing. Races take place over 200 m, 500 m, 1000 m, 6000 m and 10,000 m. Many paddlers enter sprint racing via a club and then have the choice to compete as juniors, seniors or veterans in the male or female classes.

Marathon racing

Marathon racing is an endurance event open to anyone irrespective of age or sex. The system has nine divisions, allowing you to progress so that races become progressively longer. Races can vary from as little as 6 miles to over 120 miles.

Races take place on flat-water rivers or estuaries around the year and around the country.

Polo

Kayak polo is an exciting and fast game. Two teams of five paddlers compete in a pool or on a stretch of flat water to score goals against each other. The ball can be thrown from player to player until a goal is scored by throwing the ball into a 2 m net suspended above the water at the opponent's end of the 'pitch'. Competitions are run for men and women as juniors and seniors.

Wild-water racing

Wild-water racing is an exhilarating, high-energy kayak sport. Specially designed boats are raced, against the clock, down white-water rivers above Grade 3. Races are often longer than 3 km and give spectacular high-speed action as the kayaker picks the fastest line through the waves and boulders. A three-division system allows you to progress through harder races to the level you enjoy.

Rodeo kayaking

Rodeo kayaking competitions take place throughout the year around the country and are generally light-hearted affairs. Competitors perform tricks and stunts on short sections of white water which are then marked by a panel of judges. A series of heats progress through to a final which is normally spectacular to watch, the boats performing cartwheels and spins. The competitor linking the best sequence of smooth, stylish moves is the winner.

Surf kayaking

Competitive kayak surfing is a chance to pit yourself against both competitor and surf wave. Radically designed boats perform tricks on a wave during a 20-minute heat. Runs are then scored and your best three scores dictate your position and whether you progress on to the next round and ultimately the final. Surfing provides an ideal place to refine your skills, meet new people and relax on the beach between heats.

▲ *Kayak polo*

▲ *Rodeo kayaking*

Surf kayaking ▶

Recreational kayaking

River touring

White-water touring tends to concentrate on the mountainous areas where the steep streams provide some of the most challenging rivers. Guide books exist that identify the better sections. Each river is graded using an international grading system of 1 to 6: the higher the grade, the harder the river.

Flat-water touring is not restricted to upland areas. Canals and calmer flat-water rivers enable you to explore your surroundings in a peaceful and environmentally friendly way.

Sea kayaking

Sea kayaking is the true origin of the kayak; the Inuits (Eskimos) originally used kayaks as a means to hunt and fish. Modern sea kayaks are no longer made of skin and bone, but of glass-fibre and even of plastic.

The kayak is a very seaworthy craft in experienced hands but potentially lethal in untrained hands. Whilst training takes time, it is well spent as it opens up a whole world that is inaccessible to any other craft. Caves, sea arches and isolated bays become the playground for the adventurous kayaker, and dolphins, seals and otters can be your companions.

A good book on the subject is Derek Hutchinson's *The Complete Book of Sea Kayaking* (A & C Black).

Kayaking for the disabled

Kayaking is a sport enjoyed by many people with all kinds of disabilities. Properly trained and enlightened instructors can run introductory sessions or coach you to improve your kayaking skills. Look for a qualified kayak Instructor, Senior Instructor or Coach who holds a relevant endorsement to their award. Kayaking *is* a sport for everyone and invites participation at all levels. The BCU trains staff specifically to coach kayakers with disabilities.

Warming up and down

Kayaking is a sport suitable for all ages and body types, but it is a *physical* activity. As with any physical activity, we need to prepare our bodies so we don't strain or damage ourselves. Warming up enables your body to cope more easily with the demands of any kind of activity, no matter how slight. Warming down can avoid those aches and pains the following day.

Your warm-up can start on your way to the club, in the warm environment of the car. Put the heater on (to physically warm your body) and place a rolled up towel in the small of your back as you sit on your seat (to ensure a good posture).

When you arrive at your club, park up but leave your boat on the roof rack for the moment. Take a brief, brisk walk to the river, take a look at the river to see who else is around, say your hellos and go back up to the car for your gear. If you can get changed in a warm room, leave your buoyancy aid off. If it's cold, put on an extra jumper just for the warm-up.

If you are anticipating a lot of activity you should consider going for a short run to get your heart going and to warm your body up more thoroughly before stretching.

Listed below are some good stretches appropriate to the kayaking action. It is good to stretch inside whilst you are getting dressed – a nice way of combining the stretches and making sure your gear isn't too restrictive.

● Interlace your fingers above your head with your palms upwards. Reach up to stretch your arms, shoulders and back. Push your arms back slightly for a greater stretch and hold for 15 seconds.

● Raise your arm over your head and hold the elbow with the other hand. Gently pull the elbow behind your head towards the opposite shoulder. To enhance the stretch, bend at the hips to complement the pull on the shoulder. Hold for 15 seconds.

● Stand with your feet shoulder-width apart and place your hands on your hips. Rotate from your waist and hold for 15 seconds. To enhance the stretch, try holding a paddle in front of you and repeat the exercise.

● As for the stretch, stand up but cross your legs and gently lean forwards. Stand up slowly, cross the legs the other way and repeat.

● Lie on your back. Lift one knee to your shoulder, grasp the knee with both hands and hold for 15 seconds. Relax and do the same on the other side.

● Roll over and place your hands on the ground in front of you as if doing a press-up. Straighten your arms but leave your hips on the ground and hold for 15 seconds.

▲ *Car heater on; rolled up towel in the small of the back*

▲ *Stretching routine*

41

Stretching routine

Tips

- Before stretching, ensure you are actually warm.
- Do not stretch if it hurts.
- Use a 'pre-stretch'. Do the stretch lightly before committing yourself to the 'full blown' stretch.
- Avoid bouncing. Gradually ease your limbs into the stretch; don't jerk or pull your limbs into the stretch as this can damage them.

Equipment care

If possible leave your kayak at the club. If you want to take your kayak further afield, ensure that you have a good roof rack that fits your car securely. The upturned kayak can then be strapped to the bars.

Carrying your kayak is ideal for short distances. Bend your knees, facing the bow, and slide one arm into the cockpit (towards the bow) so that your shoulder rests under the cockpit rim. Straighten your legs and off you go. Try to use your back to lift the kayak rather than your arms.

The kayak can easily be stored at home. If turned upside-down it can be left almost anywhere out of the way, but ideally it is best stored indoors. Tying it into the roof of the garage is handy and takes up little room.

If you go out on salt water you will need to rinse your kayak with fresh water to avoid corrosion of the metal fittings. If you store the boat outside you will need to let the air out of the airbags because on a hot day the air expands and can damage the bags.

Check your gear regularly for small rips and tears. Most repairs can be done with a needle, thread and neoprene glue. With good care your gear will last well, but some parts are more susceptible than others. The latex seals on your dry cag need to be rubbed with talcum powder and kept out of sunlight as much as possible.

Repeated use of the buckle on your helmet causes it to wear and it may need to be replaced from time to time. The attachment points also need to be checked to make sure they are secure, and the foam lining may also compress a little and need extra padding.

After use, rinse your gear well. If possible wash and dry it before storing it away for your next paddle.

Your car can quickly become smelly and damp if you are not careful. Seat covers are a good buy and large plastic boxes can prevent the boot from getting wet.

▲ *Use your legs to help you pick up your boat* ▲

▼ *Boxes are a good idea*

◄ *A simple, convenient strap and buckle*

Safety tips

- Never kayak alone – groups of three is the recommended minimum.
- Always wear a buoyancy aid and do it up correctly.
- Dress for the conditions; keep yourself warm.
- Learn from a qualified Instructor or Coach.

Learning tips

- Ensure that your paddling time is enjoyable, quality time.
- Practise on alternate sides, left then right – it's really worth it.
- Spend time becoming water-confident.
- Picture yourself as you paddle, and get someone to video you.
- *Quality practice*. If it's not going well, have a break and come back to it later.
- Question your teacher; get your money's worth.
- Set yourself goals; keep them just out of reach for the moment but still attainable.
- Make sure you warm up and then warm down.

Index